D0044470

YIDDISH
for DOGS

YIDDISH

Chutzpah,

Feh!,

Kibbitz,

and

More

HYPERION
NEW YORK

for DOGS

Every Word Your Canine Needs to Know

WRITTEN AND
ILLUSTRATED BY

Janet Perr

Copyright ©: 2007 Janet Perr

Photo credits:
©iStockphoto.com/Joshua Blake: hat, p. 94
©iStockphoto.com/Tom McNemar: walker, p. xiv
©iStockphoto.com/Doug Miller: popcorn, p. 74
Photodisc/Getty Images: utensils, vase, p. 2; trash can, p. 14; sign, p. 16;
Rubik's cube, p. 20; ribbon, p. 46; wine glass, p. 50; tag, p. 60;
teeth, p. 80; chess pieces, p. 82; sign, cigarette, p. 100; disguise, p. 120

All rights reserved. No part of this book may be used or reproduced in any
manner whatsoever without the written permission of the Publisher.

Printed in Mexico.

For information address Hyperion,
77 West 66th Street, New York, New York 10023-6298.

Library of Congress Cataloging-in-Publication Data

ISBN: 1-4013-0323-4
ISBN-13: 978-14013-0323-5

Hyperion books are available for special promotions, premiums, or
corporate training. For details contact Michael Rentas, Proprietary Markets,
Hyperion, 77 West 66th Street, 12th floor, New York, New York 10023,
or call 212-456-0133.

Design by Janet Perr
and Karen Minster

FIRST EDITION

10 9 8 7 6 5 4 3 2 1

For Friendly

There were a number of people
involved with this book who were instrumental
in helping me achieve my vision.

Were it not for the early support and
sense of humor of Bob Miller, this book
would not exist. Miriam Wenger, whose
encouragement, kindness, and enthusiasm
I greatly appreciated. Brian DeFiore,
Sarah Mandell, Karen Minster, Phil Rose,
and the staff at Hyperion.

Jordan, my dog wrangler at the photo shoots;
Anita, who rounded up the Greenwich
Village dogs; Beth, who contributed with
the Westchester canines; and
Harvey, whose endless knowledge of
Yiddish is unsurpassed.

Have you ever walked down the street and said to yourself, "That dog looks like a *putz*"? Do you have a friend whose dog is a *shmendrick*? Perhaps your own canine companion is a *nudnick*. Well, welcome to my life. My dog, Friendly, is the *putz* on page 88. Don't get me wrong—she's very sweet and loveable and is adored by her family—but c'mon, she has *putz* written all over her face. Even her name is ridiculous!

It started a few years ago when my boyfriend reawakened my interest in Yiddish. He grew up with fluent Yiddish spoken in his home by his grandparents. When he started using familiar words and phrases with me, I laughed, remembering my own childhood, which was filled with a mixture of fractured Yiddish and English. There was also a sprinkling of words made up by my father that were thrown into the mix, but as a child I couldn't tell the difference. Sometimes I wondered why I didn't hear Yiddish words like *mishegoss* and *ongepatchket* in school. And does anyone but my family know where *Gabunyaland* is? It's a fictitious place, dreamed up by my father, way out in the boondocks, past *East Kishnev*, which he also made up. I thought everyone spoke that way.

It wasn't until *The Joys of Yiddish* by Leo Rosten made it into my house when I was a teenager that I realized the distinction between Yiddish and English. I howled with laughter when I saw the names my father used to call me and my siblings actually in print. Words like *draykopf, nudnick, vilda chaya,* and *ungabloozen* were right there in black and white. Derogatory yet loving, they were Yiddish words! They were part of an actual language. And best of all, other people knew these words, they hadn't been made up by my father after all. Needless to say, I stopped wondering why I rarely heard these words in the outside world. I learned that they were words spoken in Jewish households . . . or so I thought. To add to my confusion, many Yiddish words have become part of our common language. Today, *shlep, shlock,* and *oy,* to name a few, are all used freely by Jews and gentiles alike.

Yiddish is a language that doesn't mince words. Think of how many words it would take to translate the word *shlub* into English. Heavy, messy, ill-mannered, untidy, rude, impolite, clumsy, stupid, unattractive—the list goes on. And with one word that sounds exactly like what it means, Yiddish nails it on the head. *Shlub.* Maybe this is why more people should speak Yiddish to their dogs, and vice versa. It's simple, nuanced, funny, and easy to understand. Trust me, pet owners and their pets aren't always listening and need a way to get through to one another that's direct and easy to get. Sit! Stay! You're a *SHLUB!*

Let's take the simple two letter word *oy,* one of the most frequently used Yiddish expressions. Not only does it cover a range of meaning, from delight and joy, to sorrow, pain, and shock but it can be calibrated in degrees by the expressiveness of the user and by its use in multiples. *Oy* we're going to the park and I'll get to run. *Oy-oy* I have to get my ears cleaned and my nails clipped today. *Oy-oy-oy* I made on the floor.

Further, *oy* is used in conjunction with other words to embellish its meaning. *Oy vey,* I knocked my dish over. *Oy gevalt,* the door locked behind me, I'm stuck outside in the rain. *Oy vey iz mir,* I can't find my way home.

Yiddish is robust in meaning and rich in history. There's nothing like it to express subtle (or not so subtle) emotions, phrases, and descriptions. So why couldn't a dog be a *tummler,* an *umglick,* or *mishuggeh*? Couldn't he *kibbitz* or be a *putz*? Or *noodge* you off the couch? I don't see why not.

YIDDISH for DOGS

Alter Kocker

ALTER KOCKER
ALL·ter KOCK·er

1. *n* a crotchety, cantankerous, crabby,
ill-natured old man

2. literally: old pooper

The closest English equivalent is "old fart,"and it
can be shortened to A.K.

I used to be able to bound up hills and run
after squirrels, not to mention my favorite
pastime, chasing the cute poodle down the
block. I would chase her till I got a good sniff.
No more, now I sit in the sun. Maybe I'll lift
my head and take a look if she goes by.
I'd whistle if I could, but it takes too much
energy. I'm such an ALTER KOCKER.

Baleboosta

BALEBOOSTA
ball·eh·BOO·sta

I. *n* an excellent homemaker, the consummate
housewife, who always goes the extra mile.
A wife with over-the-top housekeeping,
parenting, hostessing, and cooking skills.
Tireless and noncomplaining, she does it all.

I like to help out my owner, Mrs. Goldfarb,
now *she's* a BALEBOOSTA. With all she has to
do, she walks me three times a day, cooks
gourmet meals (god forbid dog food should
touch my lips), brings me to the groomer once
a week, and still has time to raise the three kids,
throw glamorous parties, and make her husband
feel like a king. The least I can do is handle the
dusting.

Boychick

BOYCHICK   BOY·chik

1. *n* affectionate term for a young boy

As the new puppy, I get all the attention. I'm so
cute, no one gets angry when I pee on the floor.
I get a new squeaky toy every time your friends
come over. The kids across the street pet and
cuddle me all the time. The first time I went to
the vet, the receptionist exclaimed, "*Oy* is he
cute, that little BOYCHICK, let me give him
a kiss." Sometimes it's just too easy.

Bubkes

BUBKES BUB·kiss

1. *n* nothing, very little, hardly anything,
a mere pittance

2. an offensively small amount compared
to the effort it took to acquire

3. literally: beans

The dinner party, last night, you had it catered.
I was dying from the smells. Filet mignon,
grilled salmon, sautéed vegetables, potatoes au
gratin. So many desserts I couldn't even count.
And what did I get? BUBKES! . . . A few pieces
of kibble.

Chazzerai

CHAZZERAI   chkaz·err·EYE

1. *n* junk, useless stuff, extraneous knickknacks, discarded castoffs

2. rotten food, literally: pig's feed

The last time we visited your mother she made us take such CHAZZERAI home with us. She should have had a yard sale! I had to squeeze into the backseat of the car, along with some old Tupperware, four mismatched coffee mugs, a broken DustBuster, an ugly lamp, a shoe box full of letters from camp, a pair of skis, and a folding card table. It was quite uncomfortable.

Chutzpah

CHUTZPAH
CHKOOTS·pah

1. *n* gall, nerve, brazenness

2. presumptuous audacity, fearless daring

Anchors away! Eureka! I'm really out on a limb now. I have no fear. I don't care what people think. I'm a dog with real CHUTZPAH. I'll jump right up onto the kitchen table while you're not looking and steal a breadstick, then disappear into thin air before you know what happened. Watch out below!

Draykopf

DRAYKOPF DRAY·cup

1. *n* a forgetful, mindless scatterbrain

2. one who might confuse you

3. literally: turn head

24-17-32? 22-17-34? *Vey iz mir!* I can't remember the combination to the lock. In one ear and out the other. What a DRAYKOPF, now I can't get into the shed. I was just looking for some old tennis balls, is that too much to ask?

Dreck

DRECK   Drek

1. *n* junk, garbage

2. literally: excrement
The closest English equivalent is "crap."

3. cheap, shoddy, poor quality
merchandise, as in "What kind of *dreck* did
you buy?"

I love to go through the garbage. God forbid
I should have something to do while you're at
work. *Oy*, the smells, heaven. Yesterday I found
a real prize, a crusty old piece of bread. Just as
I was starting to dig in, you came in the door and
cried, "What DRECK, drop it!" Couldn't you
have stayed late at a meeting?

Farchadat

FARCHADAT   Fa·CHA·ded

1. *adj* bewildered, confused, mixed-up, baffled, disoriented, perplexed—usually with an undercurrent of being overloaded and having more than one can handle, as in "It's too much"

You let me out of the house without the leash, what were you thinking? I should go out and do my business by myself? So I took off after a squirrel. How could I not? *Oy a broch*, did I get lost! I wandered around all afternoon trying to find my way home. Should I go this way, should I go that way? *Gevalt*, was I FARCHADAT.

Farshtunken

FARSHTUNKEN
far·SHTUNK·in

1. *adj*   smelly, stinky, funky

I usually love getting leftovers in my bowl, but this
time I'm not so sure. The kitchen didn't smell
so good while you were cooking. Onions, garlic,
leeks, cabbage, turnips, even brussels sprouts,
it all turned up in your FARSHTUNKEN stew.
I'll pass, and stick to my dog food tonight.

Fatootst

FATOOTST   fa·TOOTS·t

1. *adj* confused, befuddled, perplexed, discombobulated

Solving puzzles? Not my thing. Sit, stay,
lay down, roll over, that's easy.
Anything more complicated than that,
and I get all FATOOTST.

Fecrimpteh

FECRIMPTEH   fa·KRIMP·ta

1. *adj* decrepit, feeble, frail, infirm, usually
relating to an older person with aches and pains.
(Can be used as a noun as well as an adjective.
For example, a person can *be* a FECRIMPTEH
or can *have* a FECRIMPTEH back.)

Oy, my back. *Oy*, my hips. I have to walk up and
down three flights of stairs just to make? With
these FECRIMPTEH legs? You'd think we could
at least live in a building with an elevator.

Feh!

FEH! feh

1. *interj* an exclamation meaning *pee-yoo!*,
ieeeww! yuck!, usually used when one gets a whiff of
or sees something that is stinky, offensive,
or just plain icky

My nose is glued to the gutter while we go on
our walk. *Glued.* All kinds of great things fall
there. People are so careless. They drop food,
candy wrappers, dirty tissues, and their chewed
gum. Once I found a piece of a Quarter Pounder
with Cheese, I thought I hit the jackpot. To me,
this is the most exciting and purposeful part of
the day. But you? All I hear is "FEH!" and I get
a tug on the leash, like I should move on.
Move on? From these treasures?

Fress

FRESS   fress

I. *v* to eat heartily, to pig out

What can I say about FRESSING? Obviously my
favorite activity. And believe me, I'll eat anything
you put in front of me. Spaghetti with meatballs,
General Tsao's chicken, hummus and baba
ghanoush, pizza, cakes, pastries, bacon and eggs,
leftovers of all kinds. I don't discriminate.
Nothing is wasted in this house.

Gai Avek

GAI AVEK gay·a·VECK

1. an exclamation meaning "Go away!" or
"Get out of here!" or "Get lost!"

I hate it when the neighbor's dogs come over.
It's no longer just me, me, me. There they
are, jumping on the couch, nipping at my
neck, knocking my bowl over, stealing my toys.
"GAI AVEK!" I feel like yelling. Go home
already.

Gatkes

GATKES   GOT·kiz

1. *n* long underwear

I've heard this story a million times. You were a little girl growing up in Brooklyn, it was the winter of that big blizzard. Freezing, but of course, miniskirts were all the rage, regardless of the weather. You snuck out of the house and ran down the block toward school. But your mother, nothing got past her. She hollered after you for the whole neighborhood to hear, "On a day like today, you need your GATKES!" God, how embarrassing.

Geshrei

GESHREI Ga·SHRIY

1. *n* a shriek, a yell

2. a scream due to an emotional upset, usually shrill in tone

We were at an outdoor café, one of my favorite places because I can rest under the table and wait for food to drop. There I was, minding my own business, and this big dumb oaf came by and stepped on my tail. *Oy vey!* I let out the biggest GESHREI you ever heard. My family felt so sorry for me, I got half a corned beef sandwich. This tragedy should happen more often.

Goniff

GONIFF   GAH·nif

1. *n* a thief, a swindler, a crook

2. a businessman with shady dealings

The fuzzy slippers in the bedroom? Mine!
The socks left on the bathroom floor? Mine!
The dollar bill you dropped by the front door?
Mine! The baby's stuffed animal that was flung
out of the crib? Mine! You drop a cracker on
the floor? Mine! Call me a GONIFF if you wish,
but the minute it hits the floor—it's all mine!

Goyim

GOYIM   GOY·yim

1. *n* gentiles, non Jews ("goy" is singular,
"goyim" is plural, "goyishe" is the adjective form)

Every holiday season, you put me in the car with
the kids and drive around the neighborhood to
look at the Christmas lights. What those GOYIM
do to their houses! The blinking lights, the
Santas on the roof, the reindeer on the front
lawn. Can we have lights on our house too?

Kibbitz

KIBBITZ KIB·bits

1. *v* to fool around, to joke,
to tease, to bug, to pester

2. to offer unwanted commentary

Don't get me wrong, I love the attention when
the kids play with me. But sometimes it's too
much, the KIBBITZING. Poking me, pulling
my tail, making fun of me, playing monkey-in-
the-middle so I can never get the ball. And they
wonder why I nip.

Klutz

KLUTZ   kluts

1. *n* a clumsy, graceless, inept, bungling,
fumbling person

2. someone who is accident-prone

I was just running around, chasing the ball.
Did I know the door to the basement was open?
Of course not. I followed the ball as it bounced
down the stairs, losing my footing in the process.
The ball wasn't the only thing that ended up
bouncing down the stairs. I'm such a KLUTZ.

Knish

KNISH   k·nish

1. *n* a dumpling, fried or baked, with a filling most commonly of meat or potatoes

The street vendor on the corner of Seventy-second and Columbus has the best KNISHES in the city. Thank god we have to pass him twice a day on our walk to the park. The delicious morsels dropped on that corner of the sidewalk are enough to keep me happy all day.

Krenk

KRENK   crank

1. *n*   an illness, a sickness

A *farshlepteh krenk*—a chronic ailment

If it's not one thing it's the other. A rash on
the belly. Throwing up. No energy. Coughing.
A trip to the vet. The thermometer, you know
where. The antibiotics. The special dog food.
And still such a *farshlepteh* KRENK.

Kvell

KVELL   kvell

1. *v* to beam with pride, usually over
the achievement of a child

I'm the star of obedience school. They told
me to sit, I sat. They told me to come, I came.
They told me to stay, I stayed. Roll over?
No problem. And when you came to see the
progress? I performed perfectly. It was worth
the effort to see you KVELL over me.

Macher

MACHER   MA·kcher

1. *n* the leader, the boss, someone with
connections, the head honcho

I used to be the big shot at the dog park.
I was the alpha dog, dominant over all.
Then that big black dog moved in on my
territory. He acts like he's the boss.
When I see him, I lie on my back and let
him strut on by. So much for the glory days.
Now he's the big MACHER.

Maven

MAVEN MAY·vin

1. *n* an expert, a connoisseur, a person
knowledgeable in a particular area

I know you're a wine MAVEN. After the
dinner party the other night, one of your
guests left a glass on the floor so I took a sniff.
Beats me if I can tell the difference between
a Merlot and a Cabernet.

Mazel Tov

MAZEL TOV MA·zull TOFF

1. *interj* congratulations, kudos, praise

After three weeks of obedience school, I finally
learned to sit and stay. Must have been all
those dog treats. Imagine getting something to
eat every time you sat down? "MAZEL TOV,"
said the trainer, you're so smart. Smart?
I wanted the treats!

Megillah

MEGILLAH   ma·GILL·uh

1. *n* a long drawn-out story, tediously slow,
usually boring, full of tireless details

The other night when your niece came over to
stay? You were reading to her forever. It was
getting late, around 11 p.m., and I was sitting
by the door with my legs crossed, I really needed
to go out. *Oy,* and I'm listening to you drone
on and on, *blah*, *blah*, *blah*, reading the whole
MEGILLAH. Hurry up! I gotta go.

Mensch

MENSCH   mench

1. *n* a good guy, a decent person, someone to look up to and admire, a person with dignity, a person to be respected

2. a man of real character

Boy, did I luck out that day at the ASPCA when you walked in. You came right up to my kennel, patted me on the head, gave me treats, and took me directly to the "getting to know you" area, where you hugged me, kissed me, and said over and over that I was a good dog. Little did I know you also coach the Little League team, volunteer at the soup kitchen, and take your mother out to dinner every Sunday night. Such a MENSCH.

Metziah

METZIAH   met·ZEE·yuh

1. *n*   a bargain, a real find

We were out shopping for a new leash and collar
the other day. Well, I wasn't exactly shopping,
just tolerating being in the pet store with you,
standing patiently while you inspected every
item. Leather, nylon, studded, not studded,
fancy, plain. I hear you shriek, "*Gevalt,* $9.99 for
the leather? What a METZIAH, I'll take two!"

Mieskeit

MIESKEIT   MEES·kyte

1. *n* ugly, unattractive

Yup, I was born this way. Friendly, sweet, loving,
but take a good look at me, most people run in
the other direction. Thank goodness you adopted
me. My other owner, her daughter cried every
time she looked at me. "What a MIESKEIT,"
she'd say. But I won you over with affection and
my good disposition. And in return, I'll be a loyal
companion forever.

Mishmash

MISHMASH   MISH·mash

1. *n* a mix-up, a conglomeration of things

2. a jumble, a mess

So they have these fancy new dogs now, cockapoo, labradoodle, pugwahwah, a MISHMASH of different breeds. What, us normal dogs aren't good enough?

Mishpocha

MISHPOCHA
mish·POOKCH·ah

1. *n* family, extended family, relatives, clan

Fido, Lucky, Buster, Coco, and Fluffy,
they're all coming over later. We run around
like crazy and nip at each other in fun, then for
no reason we burst into song, usually old disco
tunes from the time we were litter-mates.
Buster likes "Macho Man," Fluffy is partial to
Donna Summer. Fido pees on the floor, and
Lucky throws up. MISHPOCHA, some things
never change.

Mishuggeh

MISHUGGEH
mi·SHUG·guh

1. *adj* insane, nuts, crazy, mixed-up, loony, batty, bonkers

2. *n* *mishegoss* is the noun form meaning "insanity"

The dog across the street, Sadie, stands in the driveway and chases her tail. Around and around and around she twirls. She never gives up. All day long she does this. She's MISHUGGEH.

Noodge

NOODGE nudge

1. *v* to nag, to bother, to annoy

2. *n* someone who is a pest, a pain in the neck

I was lying on the couch snoozing, and you
came over to lie with me, or so I thought.
But then you NOODGED me until I fell
onto the floor. You ended up with the whole
couch to yourself. I thought there was enough
room for both of us!

Nosh

NOSH   Nosh

1. *v* to snack, to eat a small meal, to nibble

2. *n* a bite, a cookie, a cracker, a little bit of
food between meals

Thank god when you leave for work in the
morning, you hide treats all around the house
so I can have a little NOSH during the day.
Sometimes I find a cracker under the cushion
of the couch. Once you put a piece of matzoh
on your pillow (knowing I'd jump on your bed
for my nap). And I always know to check the rug
by the front door—yesterday I found two baby
carrots. God forbid I should starve to death
while you're gone.

Nu?

NU? Noo

I. *interj* "NU?" has many meanings,
most common are "So?", "Well?"
(Other meanings include: "What's up?",
"What's new?", "How are you?", "Tell me!")

NU? Did you hear there's a new dog on the block? I saw him walk by. He's cute, fluffy, friendly, and single, I can't wait to meet him. What? You saw him too? NU-NU? You met him? *Oy Gevalt*, does he have a brother?

Nudnick

NUDNICK   NOOD·nik

1. *n* a pest, a nuisance

2. an obnoxious person

Hey, did you hear that NUDNICK in the
theater last night? He was *yap-yap-yapping* on
his cell phone and eating his popcorn louder
than I've ever heard before, bothering everyone
around him. They should have thrown him
out on his tail.

Ongepatchket

ONGEPATCHKET
OONG·ga·PATCH·kid

1. *adj* gaudy, overly done, decorated beyond normal limits

2. slapped together

Princess, your cousin's dog? Always groomed and shampooed. And the leather collar with the rhinestones, every color. Let's not forget the toenails, the most gorgeous pedicure. The leash? Matches the collar, of course. And your cousin? She has a matching leather jacket with rhinestones on the collar. Big dangly gold earrings, three large necklaces, and the baubles on each finger. The two of them, way too ONGEPATCHKET.

Oy Gevalt

OY GEVALT   oy ga·VALT

1. *interj* a cry of anguish or exclamation
similar to "Oh no" or "Uh-oh" or "Dear me"

"Oy" can be used on its own or as
part of a phrase to distinguish different
levels of catastrophe. *Oy gevalt*:"Oh goodness,"
Oy vey: "Oh, woe," or the extended
Oy vey iz mir: "Oh, woe is me."

OY GEVALT, I better get out of the way.
A disaster is about to strike. I feel like
something's going to happen. What could
it be? A major calamity? *Oy vey iz mir.*

Pisk

PISK   pisk

1. *n* big mouth, loud mouth

She bursts in suddenly, the dog walker, barking
orders at me (no pun intended). "Hi, Fluffy!",
"Do you want to go for a walk?", "Get your
leash!", "Get your toy!", "Come on, let's go",
"Fluffy, let's go out!", "Come on, Fluffy, come
on, come on, come on!" All my peace and quiet,
gone. What a PISK she has on her!

Pitsel

PITSEL   PIT·sell

1. *n* a little bit, a little piece

Sometimes you treat me like a pawn on
a chessboard. You control my every move,
telling me to sit, stay, lie down, roll over.
What, I have no power here? I'm just a
little PITSEL? I thought I was the pack leader!

Plotz

PLOTZ   plots

I. *v* to burst with emotion, practically to the point of passing out

You got the T-bone steak? Just for me?
Because it's my birthday? I'm PLOTZING!

Pupik

PUPIK   PUP·ick

1. *n* belly button

You took me for a walk the other day. *Vey iz mir*,
I was so embarrassed, such a short-cropped shirt
and low-rise jeans you had on. That's fine for
your granddaughter, but you? Hello! Your
PUPIK was showing! And that belly-button ring,
what were you thinking?

Putz

PUTZ putts

1. *n* (offensive) a jerk, an ass, an idiot, a fool,
a moron, a term of contempt

So I was in the park, it was a gorgeous day,
mind you, all the pretty girls were out for a walk.
And there she was—the cutest white poodle,
with a pink bow on top of her head. I went right
over to sniff her, but she was having none of it.
"Leave me alone, you PUTZ," she said as she
turned and trotted away. Well! She's not the only
fish in the sea.

Sha!

SHA!   shah

1. *interj* (said softly) "Quiet, please"

2. (said loudly) "Shut up!"

On the occasion that you drop me at Doggie
Day Care, it's really not so bad. I'd rather be
home, but I know you'll be working late or
otherwise engaged, and it's kind of fun sniffing
all the dogs. But let me tell you, once one starts
barking, they all start barking, like a chain
reaction. "SHA!", says the attendant to the
group, to no avail. Big dogs, little dogs, fat dogs,
thin dogs, fierce dogs, compliant dogs, such a
cacophony of sounds. You could lose your mind.

Shandeh

SHANDEH   SHAN·duh

I. *n* a disgrace, a shame

I know . . . I peed on the floor during
your dinner party. "Such a SHANDEH,"
you declared. The thing is, everyone was
feeding me under the table. How could
I possibly tear myself away to go outside,
even for a minute?

Shaygets

SHAYGETS SHAY·gitz

1. *n* a non-Jewish young man

2. a wild boy, a rascal

Did you have to dress me up at holiday time
with the red cap and the white beard and make
me stand next to a sack of gifts? I look like a
little SHAYGETS. What were you thinking?
I was so embarrassed. Next, you'll have me
singing carols and pulling a sleigh!

Shayna Maidel

SHAYNA MAIDEL
SHAY·na MAY·dul

1. pretty girl (*shayna adj*: pretty; *maidel n*: girl;
also, *shayna punim*: pretty face)

I, ya know, like, went to the groomer? They did
my nails, pink, no less. And the shampoo!
Ooooh, I smell like lavender. The ribbon?
In my hair? It's so cool, much nicer than my
friend's. Hers wasn't even silk, can you, like,
imagine? And when they dropped me off at
home? Well, like, everyone exclaimed, "*Zaya*
SHAYNA MAIDEL" . . . "Such a pretty girl!"

Shiksa

SHIKSA   SHICK·sah

1. *n* a non-Jewish young woman

Your new girlfriend? The SHIKSA?
Gevalt is she adorable! And showers me with
affection every time she visits. Slim, blond,
young, with a cute little upturned nose . . .
Your mother is going to kill you!

Shlemiel

SHLEMIEL shla·MEEL

1. *n* a loser, a dope, a fool

Only a real bona fide SHLEMIEL would smoke
a cigarette in front of a NO SMOKING sign.
Not to mention the cancer and the lung
problems, let alone the smell, and the cost of
course, $4.50 a pack, nothing to sneeze at.

Shlep

SHLEP   shlep

1. *v* to drag, to carry, usually taking some effort and involving too many heavy items

2. *n* (*shlepper*) a lazy or inefficient person, an incompetent

What, your legs are broken? *Oy*, I'm straining my back, you're so heavy. How come I have to SHLEP you home?
You can't walk?

Shlock

SHLOCK   shlock

1. *n* a cheaply made item, of poor or
inferior quality

2. a defective article

So you bought a cheap watch at the discount
store? What do you expect, that it won't fall
apart? It's a piece of SHLOCK, not a Rolex,
for heaven's sake.

Shlub

SHLUB   shlub

1. *n* a clumsy slob, an oaf, a boorish,
graceless person

Oy, that delivery guy. What a SHLUB. He comes
in with grease dripping from the pizza box and
mud on his shoes, shirt untucked, belly hanging
out. Ashes falling all over from his cigar.
And remember last month? He tripped on the
edge of the rug on the way in. The meatball
heroes went flying. The bags of chips. It's a
good thing I was underfoot to help clean it up.
I didn't mind at all.

Shluffin

SHLUFFIN   SHLOOF·in

1. *v* sleeping, napping

That square of sunlight on the living room floor? That's my spot, all day long. I lie there SHLUFFIN, not a care in the world. Heaven.

Shmatte

SHMATTE SHMAT·tah

1. *n* a rag

2. an inferior article of clothing

You use the same old SHMATTE to clean up spills. It's really gross. There are these things called sponges, you know. Or paper towels, god forbid.

Shmear

SHMEAR   shmeer

1. *v* to spread, to smear

2. *n* a spread of some sort, usually cream cheese

It's the Sunday morning ritual, lox and bagels
from Zabar's. All I get is my dry dog food?
Could I at least get a SHMEAR of the canned
food on top? Or a little chopped liver, that
would be even better.

Shmendrick

SHMENDRICK
SHMEN·drick

1. *n*   a jerk, a dork, a boob, a wimp

2. *adj*   weak, lame, physically small

Could also be used affectionately
to describe a child

I sniff here, I sniff there. I pull you up the
block, I pull you down the block. I'm looking
for the perfect place to do my business. You
think I'm gonna go, but then I'm not quite
ready. You think I found the right spot, but
then I change my mind. It starts to rain, you're
getting wet, I haven't gone yet. Maybe that spot,
no *that* spot, no over there. You've lost your
patience and yell, "Go already, you
SHMENDRICK! You think I have all day?"

Shmutz

SHMUTZ   shmuts

1. *n* dirt

I was digging and digging in the backyard.
What was I looking for? Who knows?
The digging is so much fun. The dirt flinging
all around, flying through my legs, my face
buried in the hole. What's down there?
A woodchuck? An ant? A buried treasure?
You called my name, I picked my head up out
of the hole, and you shrieked, "*Oy*, you're
covered in SHMUTZ!"

Shnorrer

SHNORRER   SHNORE·er

1. *n*   A beggar, a moocher, a chiseler, a leech

I hate it when Cooper comes over. He sticks his
nose in my bowl and finishes my food, the food
I save for later. He chews on my favorite rawhide
bone, the one with "real" beef flavor. He lies in
my bed, the round one from KMart, and sheds
all over the cushion. What a SHNORRER he is.
Next he'll be asking for spare change.

Shnozz

SHNOZZ   shnoz

1. *n* nose, usually large and not attractive

Having a big SHNOZZ comes in handy when
I'm sniffing my way around the neighborhood.
All those dogs. All those smells. I know who has
passed by and where they're going. I know if
they lingered or rushed by. As plain as the nose
on my face.

Shtumma

SHTUMMA   SHTUM·mah

1. *adj*   quiet, silent, speechless

When we're at the vet your mouth doesn't stop.
"He's not eating much, there's a bump on his
elbow, his eyes look watery, are his teeth OK?
Is his coat dull? Are his nails too long? Does he
need shots? Heartworm pills?" And the doctor . . .
SHTUMMA. He knows I'm fine.

Shvitz

SHVITZ   shvits

I. *v* to sweat, perspire

It was time for my walk, I had to make, but it was the middle of August in New York City . . . *Gevalt,* the heat! The sizzling sidewalk! Ninety-five degrees and humid. It's like an oven, the summer. Can you imagine what it's like when you're six inches from the asphalt? By the time we got to the end of the block I was SHVITZING and yanking on the leash to get back into the air-conditioning. Such torture just to go to the bathroom.

Spritz

SPRITZ   sprits

1. *n* a brief spray of liquid, a quick squirt

2. *v* to spray, to squirt

Do you know how to get me to stop barking when the doorbell rings? You think a SPRITZ of warm water in the face will startle me and I'll stop the barking. Oh yeah? What are you, nuts? It's a game. I like to bite the water midair and I'll bark even more when you SPRITZ me again.

TCHOTCHKE
CHOCH·kee

1. *n* knickknack, bric-a-brac, trinket
2. literally: treasure

Tchotchke

I had so much fun at that yard sale. I kept swiping
TCHOTCKES off the table and burying them
in the dirt. I didn't understand why I kept getting
shooed away. I thought I was helping.

Traif

TRAIF   trayf

1. *n* any food that is not kosher, for example shellfish and bottom-feeders

2. any animal with a cloven hoof, or not slain according to rabbinical law

It's here, the Chinese food. I can't wait for the leftovers. The shrimp with lobster sauce, to die for. The spare ribs, I lose my mind. And the roast pork fried rice, oh my god. Such TRAIF!

Tsura

TSURA   TSEWER·a

I. *n* a minor issue, usually medical, that starts
out benign and is made worse by the foolish
actions of the individual

I had a little itch but after scratching it constantly
for two days, it turned into such a big TSURA
that it got infected and I had to go to the vet for
treatment. And now, on top of the itching, it
hurts. And the vet bill, you could have a heart
attack.

Tsuris

TSURIS   TSEWER·is

1. *n* troubles, worries, woes

Here I am at Camp Canine. You went to Europe
for a week. You think I could have a nice
relaxing time in this fancy place? No, of course
not. Have I got TSURIS. The food is different,
not my regular. The dog in the kennel next to
me barks all night. And on top of it all, they
make me exercise twice a day. *Oy vey,* I can't wait
till you get back.

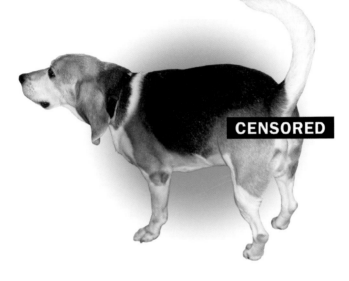

Tuchus

TUCHUS   TOOK·us

1. *n* rear end, behind, derriere

If I keep eating so much food, my TUCHUS is going to get so big, I won't be able to fit through the door! But then, of course, there will be more of me to love.

Tummler

TUMMLER   TUM·ler

1. *n* the master of ceremonies, an entertainer

2. someone who makes a racket

I was just napping in the sun, minding my own business, when the TUMMLER from next door trotted in like a hurricane, barking, looking for toys, and spinning around doing tricks. He tried to get me to join him, but all I could manage was to lift my head off the floor. I wasn't giving up my spot in the sun for these hysterics.

Umglick

UMGLICK   UMM·glick

1. *n* a born loser

2. an unlucky individual

Yesterday morning my tail got caught in the
door, then I stubbed my paw on the edge of the
coffee table. That was after I knocked over my
water bowl by accident. I'm such an UMGLICK.
But today I found a lottery ticket on the street.
Maybe my luck is changing.

Ungabloozen

UNGABLOOZEN
OONG·ga·BLOOZ·en

1. *v* pouting, sulking, brooding

I sat all afternoon in the corner UNGABLOOZEN.
It was a dreary, gloomy day, and I was wishing it
would stop raining. Nothing could cheer me up—
not treats, not scratching behind my ears,
not fetching the ball in the house. I wanted to
go outside and chase squirrels.

Vilda Chaya

VILDA CHAYA
VIL·duh CKHAI·ya

1. *n* wild animal

2. common usage: describes a child who runs
around making a commotion

The moment I tear through the door of your
mother's apartment I take off after her cat,
knocking over a vase, and bumping up against
the hutch with the good china in it. Then to
quench my thirst, I take a drink of water out of
the toilet. "Oh, I see you brought the VILDA
CHAYA with you!" she says.

Vontz

VONTZ   vonts

1. *n* affectionate expression for a
mischievous child

2. literally: bedbug

I felt an itch, only to see a little VONTZ
crawling away from me. And I don't mean
your nephew, that pain in the neck, always
pulling my tail. I know what I saw.

Yenta

YENTA   YEN·tuh

1. *n* a busybody, a gossip, one who
spreads scandals

I heard from that YENTA across the street,
that you've got buns in the oven, if you know
what I mean. And who's the lucky father?
Oh, you're not sure?

Yontiff

YONTIFF   YUNN·tiff

1. *n*   a holiday

Literally: good day

It's YONTIFF again. Time to cook the meal, invite the relatives over. On Hanukkah we light the menorah, on Purim I'm dressed like Queen Esther. I love the holidays. I get leftover brisket, lots of petting from guests, and everyone showers me with gifts.

Zaftig

ZAFTIG ZAFF·tig

1. *adj* plump, buxom, beefy, full-figured, well rounded

2. literally: juicy

Mmm . . . food, I love to eat. Give me dog food, leftovers, treats. Last week's Chinese food? I'll take it. Those cheap treats from the supermarket? Fine with me. The crumbs that fall on the floor? I'll clean it up. I'll eat just about anything, and with gusto. So what if I'm a little ZAFTIG? I love myself just the way I am, and you should too.

Photographing the dogs for this book was pure joy, truly a labor of love. Every dog in this book was adored and treated like a member of the family, exalted and fawned over. Every person who participated was an ardent dog lover as well as a good sport, and knew their dog might appear as anything from a *shayna maidel* to a *shlub*. A heartfelt thanks goes out to all of you, for your good nature, sense of humor, and enthusiasm in helping me with this project.

All of the dogs in this book were photographed "au naturel." Any visual enhancement was done through collage and retouching. And, of course, no dogs were harmed in the making of this book. On the contrary, they were smothered with love, scratched on the head, kissed, and given plenty of dog treats.

Many of the people whom I visited offered to dress their dog up in all sorts of clothes and props. One person even had a little yarmulke and tallis because her dog had been bar mitzvahed. Another appeared with a teeny motorcycle jacket. Bandanas, booties, sweaters, fancy collars, you name it— all were dragged out of the closet. None were needed.

Almost everyone wanted their dog to perform in some way, to show off for me. "Sit" and "stay" were the most common commands. What smart dogs! We were all *kvelling*! And almost *everyone* asked if their dog had to be Jewish to participate. Absolutely not! Yiddish is for everyone.

Sadly, four dogs in this book, Buster, Mikey, Ella, and my own dear Friendly, are no longer with us. Hopefully, we can all find comfort in the fact that they will be immortalized forever as the *fecrimpteh* dog, the dog with *shmutz* on his head, the *shamas* on the menorah in *yontiff*, and the *putz*, respectively.

And lastly, I'd like to thank each and every dog who gave up a half hour of their afternoon to be photographed by me. I know they would rather have been lying in the sun or running after a ball in the park, but they sat willingly and without embarrassment and were all good dogs.

A scratch behind the ears to (in alphabetical order): Abby F., Abby J., Abby M., Amelia, Annie, Banjo, Bear, Betty, Billy, Bonnie, Booker, Buddy, Buster K., Buster P., Chico, Coco, Cooper, Diana, Dinky, Dolly, Dottie, Ella, Finn, Freddy, Friendly, Hank, Harry, Imus, Jazmin, Kaylee, Keiko, Lola G., Lola J., Louis, Madelane, Malone, Mattie, Max, Maxie, Mikey, Monster, Nike, Nuri, Peppy, Quincy, Rex, Rita, Rocky, Rosie R., Rosie S., Sadie M., Sadie S., Sammy T., Sammy W., Simon, Sky, Spice, Sushi, Taja, Trina, Woody, Yoshi, and Zachary.